Graphs

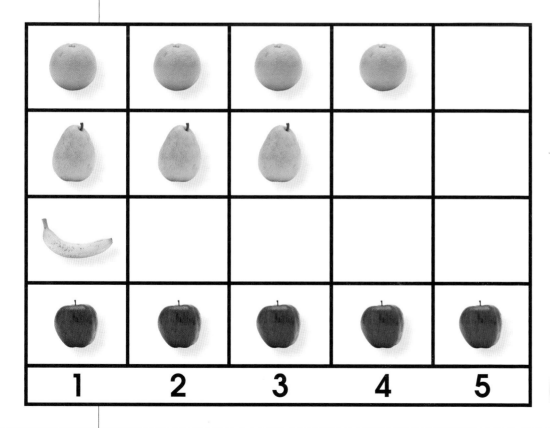

BY SARA PISTOIA

The Child's World

Published by The Child's World®
1980 Lookout Drive • Mankato, MN 56003-1705
800-599-READ • www.childsworld.com

Acknowledgments
The Child's World®: Mary Berendes, Publishing Director
The Design Lab: Design
Editing: Jody Jensen Shaffer

Photographs ©: BrandXPictures: 18; PhotoDisc: 20;
all other images David M. Budd Photography.

ISBN 9781623235307
LCCN 2013931353

Printed in the United States of America
Mankato, MN
July, 2013
PA02173

ABOUT THE AUTHOR

Sara Pistoia is a retired elementary teacher living in Southern California with her husband and a variety of pets. In authoring this series, she draws on the experience of many years of teaching first and second graders.

Graphs

A **graph** is a way of keeping track when we **sort** and **count** things. It lets us see quickly how many things we have. It helps us **compare** numbers of different things, too.

How many crayons of each color do we have? We can use a graph to see.

We can lay out the crayons just as this **picture graph** shows. Now we can see how many crayons of each color we have.

It's easy to see that we have **more** red crayons than yellow or green crayons.

Are there **fewer** yellow crayons than green or red ones?

yellow	yellow	yellow	yellow			
green	green	green	green	green		
red	red	red	red	red	red	red
1	2	3	4	5	6	7

What can we say about the fruit in this bowl? What could we do to learn more? How could we show others what we learn?

Let's sort, count, and graph!

First, sort the fruit by kind. Then, count how many there are of each kind. Then we can make a graph!

Let's compare the different fruits by looking at the graph. Four words will help us: more, fewer, **most**, and **least**.

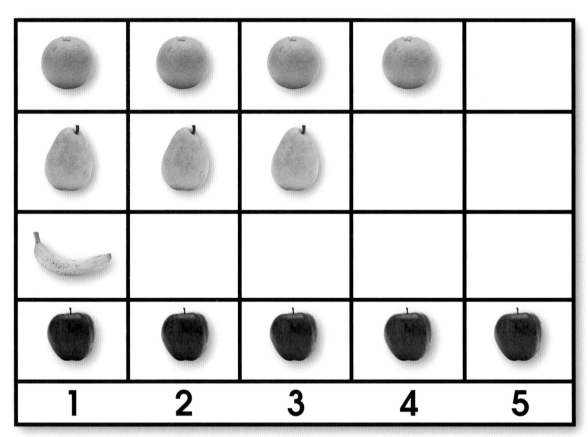

Do we have more apples or oranges?

Do we have fewer pears or bananas?

Of which fruit do we have the most?

Of which fruit do we have the least?

We can make a graph of this jar of cookies, too.
What would you like to find out about them?

Would you like to know which kind has the most?
Which kind has the least?

This **bar graph** has pictures on one side. The pictures show the different kinds of cookies. As we count each cookie, we shade a square in that row. The numbers across the bottom show how many we have counted.

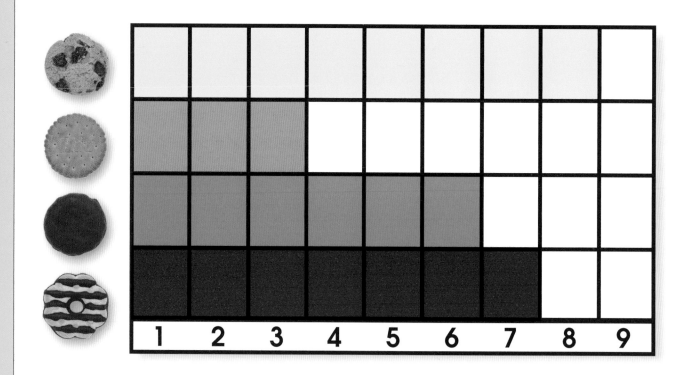

The bar graph can help us answer lots of questions.

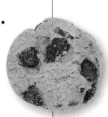

Were there more striped cookies or chocolate-chip cookies?

There were more fudge cookies than butter cookies. But how many more?

Wow! There are more chocolate-chip cookies here than any other kind!

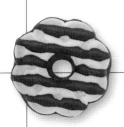

Here is another bar graph. This one tells us about jelly beans. The bar for the red jelly beans ends on square 8. The bar for the green jelly beans ends on square 4.

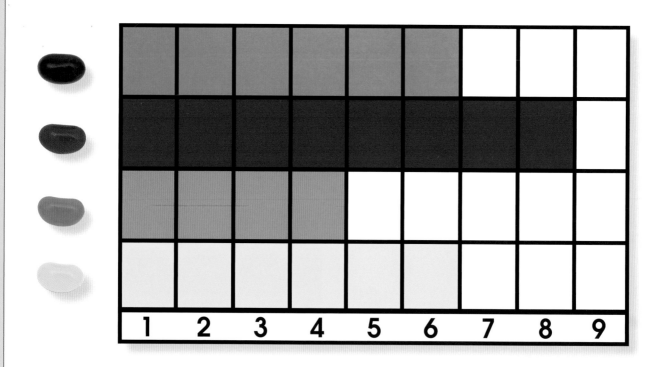

Look at the graph. How many more red jelly beans than green jelly beans are there?

There are four more red jelly beans than green ones. We have the same number of black and yellow jelly beans.

A **line graph** is another kind of graph. We can use it to keep track of something over a period of time.

How does this baker keep track of the bread he sells each day? He uses a line graph.

The next page shows how the baker keeps track of the bread he sells.

The purple line is for the bread the baker sold last week.

On which day did he sell the most?

On which day did he sell the least?

The baker's best day was Friday. He sold 70 loaves of bread that day.

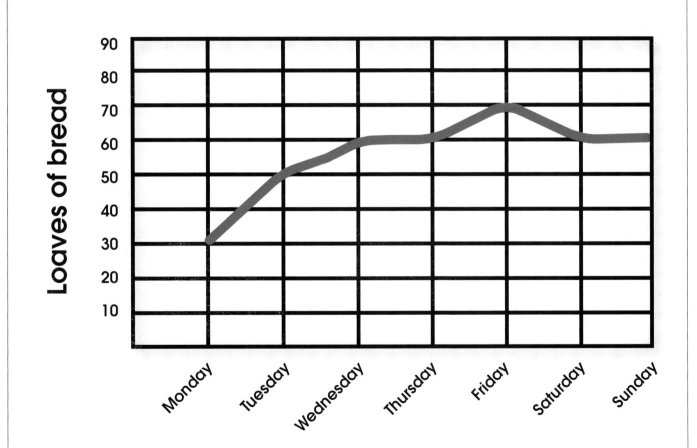

The school nurse uses graphs, too. Her graph keeps track of how many students she has seen.

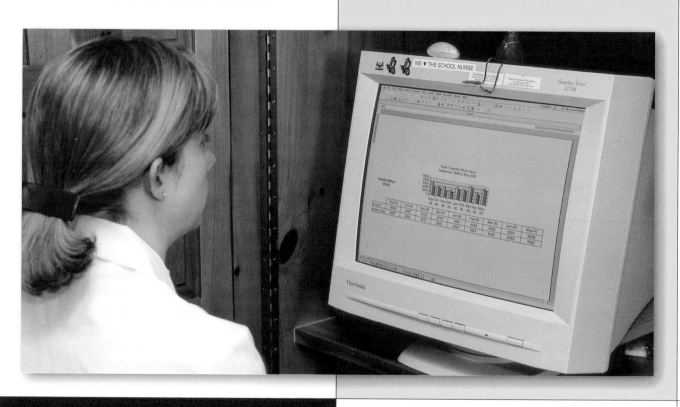

A teacher can use a graph to show students how well they are doing in class.

Graphs are useful tools for many people, no matter what they sort or count.

Key Words

bar graph

compare

count

fewer

graph

least

line graph

more

most

picture graph

sort

Index